POSSESSED

The Amityville Horror Enigma

by

Matthew Hutton

First published
2018

Goatshead Castle
Productions

caput inter nubila condit

ISBN: 9781980401285

"I heard a rather deep voice behind me saying, 'Get out!' It seemed so directed toward me..."

(Father Ralph J. Pecoraro)

"People ask me why I stayed in the house as long as I did. But the house had a strange comfort to it. Once you were inside, you did not want to leave. It was, after all, our home. Yet it affected everyone who entered it."

(George Lutz - March 26, 1980)

Introduction

I remember quite vividly reading Jay Anson's novel *The Amityville Horror* when I was still a teenager at School.   Living in the UK I had no idea what the characters looked like, or for that matter what the house looked like, other than the vague blueprints which were contained within the pages of the book. Nevertheless, the words of the manuscript started me on a course which lead me to become a journalist and later the Assistant Editor of a London based monthly Newspaper called *Psychic World*.   And over the years I became well versed in all the aspects of the Amityville haunting, and the tragic murders which preceded it, although I must admit, it was the latter hauntings which captured my interest. So when the opportunity presented itself to interview one of the children who lived in the house, 'Christopher Lutz' (known today as *Christopher John Quaratino*), I jumped at the chance.

This book is therefore partly based upon my own research and observations, and partly based upon the information given to me by Christopher Lutz (aka Quaratino), who along with his brother Daniel and sister Melissa, are now the only people living, who can offer any sort of accurate insight in to what life was like living in probably the most famous, or *infamous*, haunted homes ever recorded.

Following these interviews I wrote a series of articles for *Psychic World Newspaper* (published issues #213 November 2011 and #221   July 2012), which are incorporated in this script.

As a footnote, I would like to state that my objective in writing this work, was not to debunk, support or draw more unwanted confusion to the original claims made by George and Kathleen Lutz.   However, if what Christopher told me is true (and I have no reason to doubt him). Then we have to start thinking of the house as a '*tool*' used in much the same way as one would use an Ouija board to open a doorway of communication between this world and the next. And just like an Ouija board,   once   you   open   the   door   of communication, you have no way of policing who, or what, comes through.

The main problems with the haunting on Ocean Avenue, is that it has been embroidered and fictionalised since the story first broke. Today the true facts of the murders and the shadowing haunting, have been buried under four decades of of myths, misinterpretation and sometimes just outright lies. Like some twisted game of Chinese Whispers, these falsehoods concerning the house keep getting carried and copied from article to article, website to website and movie to movie.
With endless books and articles regarding the house, and a staggering ten movies using the premise (along with the name), most of which are completely fictitious; such as the *Amityville Horror: the Lost Tapes*, or *Shattered Hopes* which claims to offer new evidence about the murders. It is no wonder that most people, and even serious researches in to the paranormal, have problems piecing together what really took place in that house.

In the following pages I will try to clarify some of the facts and bury the myths. It is my hope that readers will find something new, or at the very least, look at the haunting from a different angle. And in an attempt to add some flesh to the bones of this manuscript, I have used as many relevant photographic images as possible.

Amityville Property Map

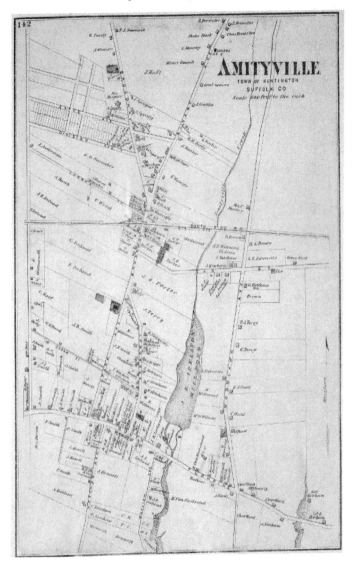

History of 112 Ocean Avenue

According the deeds and information compiled by the Amityville Historical Society, the location of the house on Ocean Avenue had once been farmland belonging to the Ireland family, one of Amityville's most prominent and influential residents.

There is a curious article within the *New York Times* archive dating back to the late 1800s, following a number of dead babies were discovered in the Amityville Creek. These babies were in all likelihood fetuses – in a later article it is revealed that a woman, with the surname Ireland from Ocean Avenue, was charged with "perverting nature" which we today would class as illegal abortions.

While it cannot be verified if this is any relation of the then owners of the house, if not related - it is a very strange coincident.

What we do know is that on January 14, 1924, Annie Ireland sold the existing property to John and Catherine Moynahan.

However before we move on, there is another *coincidence* which can be found in an article of the New York Herald, dated 1887 under the heading of 'Haunted House' which reads: *Amityville Posses a 'Haunted House.'*

"No none knows why it is called so, but it is known as such, and that settles it. It is a place of valuable property, situated on the banks of a pretty lake half mile from the beach.

"It was bought some years ago by a New York party, who fixed it up handsomely and prepared it for occupancy in every way, but never occupied it and has ever since let it go to ruin.

"Its vast garden is full of wild weeds: portico has become rickety; its Grecian columns are tumbling down, and its general appearance is weird and forsaken."

New York Herald, 1887

This has some remarkable similarity (haunted and location) to the house of today - Only ninety years earlier.

A year following the purchase by John and Catherine Moynahan, a builder, (Jesse Perdy) was hired and constructed the large Dutch Colonial style house which we are all familiar with.

Perdy built the house above the foundations of the much older and smaller house that once stood on the land. The Moynahan's relocated this smaller one-story house further down the street, where it still stands today.

When John and Catherine Moynahan died, their daughter Eileen Fitzgerald, took over the property and lived in the house for many years with her own family until October 17, 1960, when John and Mary Riley bought the house.

The Riley's daughter is the Christine Belford, the actress who appeared in countless TV shows in America, and is probably best remembered for playing Susan Farragut in the television soap *Dynasty*, and her role as Eliza in the 1983 movie adaptation of Stephen King's book *Christine*.

Christine lived in the house for approximately five years (between the age 11 until age 16), with her parents, who because of marital problems divorced and sold the house to the DeFeo family on June 28, 1965.

At this point 112 Ocean Avenue was gifted the somewhat ironic name of *High Hopes*. By the new owners.

Actress Christine Belford (1973)

Belford Lived at 112 Ocean Avenue as a teenager

The DeFeo family lived in the house for more than nine years until November 13, 1974, when all but one of their lives was cut short.

At 6:30pm on that fateful day, Ronald DeFeo Jr ran in to his local public house (Henry's Bar), in what appeared to be a frantic state, exclaiming:

"Please! You've got to help me! I think my mother and father are shot!"

Defoe then, accompanied by his friend, Robert "Bobby" Kelske, John Altieri, Joey Yeswit, William Scordmaglia and Al Saxton, drove back to the house on Ocean Avenue where they discovered the front door unlocked – the lights switched off and the family dog *Shaggy*, tied to the inside of the kitchen's back door barking.

They also found the dead bodies of the DeFeo family. Following the discovery, Joey Yeswit called the police.

The following is a complete transcript of the Phone Call:

Operator: This is Suffolk County Police. May I help you?"

Yeswit: "We have a shooting here. Uh, DeFeo."

Operator: "Sir, what is your name?"

Yeswit: "Joey Yeswit."

Operator: "Can you spell that?"

Yeswit: "Yeah. Y-E-S W I T."

Operator: "Y-E-S . . ."

Yeswit: "Y-E-S-W-I-T."

Operator: ". . . W-I-T. Your phone number?"

Yeswit: "I don't even know if it's here. There's, uh, I don't have a phone number here."

Operator: "Okay, where you calling from?"

Yeswit: "It's in Amityville. Call up the Amityville Police, and it's right off, uh . . .Ocean Avenue in Amityville."

Operator: "Austin?"

Yeswit: "Ocean Avenue. What the ... ?"

Operator: "Ocean ... Avenue? Off where?"

Yeswit: "It's right off Merrick Road. Ocean Avenue."

Operator: "Merrick Road. What's ... what's the problem, Sir?"

Yeswit: "It's a shooting!"

Operator: "There's a shooting. Anybody hurt?"

Yeswit: "Ah?"

Operator: "Anybody hurt?"

Yeswit: "Yeah, it's uh, uh -- everybody's dead."

Operator: "Whattaya mean, everybody's dead?"

Yeswit: "I don't know what happened. Kid come running in the bar. He says everybody in the family was killed, and we came down here."

Operator: "Hold on a second, Sir."

(Police Officer now takes over call)

Police Officer: "Hello."

Yeswit: "Hello."

Police Officer: "What's your name?"

Yeswit: "My name is Joe Yeswit."

Police Officer: "George Edwards?"

Yeswit: "Joe Yeswit."

Police Officer: "How do you spell it?"

Yeswit: "What? I just ... How many times do I have to tell you? Y-E-S-W-I-T."

Police Officer: "Where're you at?"

Yeswit: "I'm on Ocean Avenue.

Police Officer: "What number?"

Yeswit: "I don't have a number here. There's no number on the phone. "

Police Officer: "What number on the house?"

Yeswit: "I don't even know that."

Police Officer: "Where're you at? Ocean Avenue and what?"

Yeswit: "In Amityville. Call up the Amityville Police and have someone come down here. They know the family."

Police Officer: "Amityville."

Yeswit: "Yeah, Amityville."

Police Officer: "Okay. Now, tell me what's wrong."

Yeswit: "I don't know. Guy come running in the bar. Guy come running in the bar and said there -- his mother and father are shot. We ran down to his house and everybody in the house is shot. I don't know how long, you know. So, uh . . ."

Police Officer: "Uh, what's the add ... what's the address of the house?"

Yeswit: "Uh, hold on. Let me go look up the number. All right. Hold on. One-twelve Ocean Avenue, Amityville."

Police Officer: "Is that Amityville or North Amityville?"

Yeswit: "Amityville. Right on ... south of Merrick Road."

Police Officer: "Is it right in the village limits?"

Yeswit: "It's in the village limits, yeah."

Police Officer: "Eh, okay, what's your phone number?"

Yeswit: "I don't even have one. There's no number on the phone. "

Police Officer: "All right, where're you calling from? Public phone?"

Yeswit: "No, I'm calling right from the house, because I don't see a number on the phone."

Police Officer: "You're at the house itself?"

Yeswit: "Yeah."

Police Officer: "How many bodies are there?"

Yeswit: "I think, uh, I don't know -- uh, I think they said four."

Police Officer: "There's four?"

Yeswit: "Yeah."

Police Officer: "All right, you stay right there at the house, and I'll call the Amityville Village P.D., and they'll come down."

Within ten minutes of the call, Officer Kenneth Greguski of the Amityville Village Police Department arrived at house to find the men all outside waiting on the lawn.

The police discovered six members of the DeFeo family had been murdered in the house - John Matthew DeFeo, aged 9 (*born October 24, 1965*). Marc Gregory DeFeo aged 12 (*born September 4, 1962*). Allison Louise DeFeo, aged 13 (*born August 16, 1961*). Dawn Terese DeFeo aged 18 (*born July 29, 1956*). And their parents Louise Brigante DeFeo aged 42 and Ronald Joseph DeFeo Sr, aged 43.

The murders appeared to have had some peculiar qualities, as each of the family members were shot while seemingly still in their sleep, face down on the bed.

The eldest son of the family, Ronald DeFeo Jr (nicknamed *Butch*), who initially reported the murders, told police that when he arrived home from work on the evening of November 13th, that he discovered someone had broken into the house and killed every member of his family. He later changed this claim when during the forensic investigation it was revealed that the murders had occurred in the morning.

Ronald DeFeo Jr then claimed that a man named Louis Falini (now thought to be a pseudonym of Tony Mazzeo), had arrived at the house with an accomplice, on the morning of November 13th, and had put a gun to his head and forced him to watch the two men kill his family. This claim was also proven to be false, and eventually, DeFeo confessed, stating:

"Once I started, I just couldn't stop.
It went so fast."

During his trial in November of 1975, DeFeo stated that "voices" told him to commit the murders, his lawyer, William Weber even had a psychiatrist testifying that DeFeo had a 'dissociative disorder', which indicates that Ronald would have experienced the murders as if he was outside his body or "watching" it happen, rather than experiencing himself carrying out the murders.

The prosecution also produced a psychiatrist, who argued that DeFeo actually had 'antisocial personality disorder' which meant he would have been perfectly aware of what he was doing, but just had no regard for what was right or wrong.

Ronald DeFeo Jr was found guilty of six counts of second-degree murder and sentenced to six consecutive life sentences... And his story has changed repeatedly over the past four decades.

According to one interview he gave in 1986, he claimed that his sister Dawn killed their father, after which their mother killed Dawn and the other children before turning the gun on herself?   In 1990 he claimed that Dawn shot the majority of the DeFeo's before he himself killed Dawn; and he maintains that his lawyer, William Weber, pressured him into the insanity defence they pushed at his trial. Regardless, his requests for parole have all been denied.

The DeFeo Family

Ronald DeFeo Jr 'Butch' pictured front – far right

"I think that denial of the existence of this stuff is what *it* seeks to have happen"

George Lutz (April 12th 2005)

George and Kathy Lutz

A rare photograph of Kathy in her waitress uniform, taken at Ocean Avenue while viewing the house for the first time.

In the book *'Our Haunted Lives'* *by* Jeff Belanger (which features the stories of dozens of people who have witnessed the supernatural firsthand), George Lutz says:

"If I recall correctly, this was sometime maybe late August or September, somewhere in there. We saw the house and as soon as Kathy walked in she just started smiling."

112 Ocean Avenue, stood empty for thirteen months until George and Kathy Lutz purchased the house for the unbelievably cheap price of just $80,000.

They were already aware of gruesome history of the property, but had decided that this was not an issue and the house itself would be a good investment.

The Lutz Family

George   Kathy

Christopher   Daniel   Missy

On December 18, 1975, the newly-weds along with Kathy's three children from a previous marriage (Daniel aged 9, Christopher aged 7 and Melissa aged 5), moved in to the six-bedroom house, which boasted of a swimming pool and boathouse. In addition to this (as stated in the first chapter of Anson's book), the furniture that had been in the house when Ronald DeFeo, Jr. committed the murders was reportedly still in there. George paid an additional $400 to keep it, which again was a bargain price.

According to some, the furniture was still in the exact same places it had been the night of the murders.

Maybe because of this, but more obviously because of the previous murders, the Lutzes decided to ask a Catholic Priest, Father Ralph J. Pecoraro (referred to in the original book and movie as *Father Mancusco*) to bless their new home.

The movie also depicted the priest being swarmed by flies, which never happened. However, Father Ralph J. Pecoraro did confirm during an interview in 1979, that:

"I was blessing the sewing room - It was cold. It was really cold in there. I'm like, 'Well, gee, this is peculiar,' because it was a lovely day out, and it was winter, yes, but it didn't account for that kind of coldness. I was also sprinkling holy water, and I heard a rather deep voice behind me saying, 'Get out!' It seemed so directed toward me that I was really quite startled. I felt a slap at one point on the face. I felt somebody slap me, and there was nobody there."

This incident transpired while the Lutzes were still unloading their belongings from the removal van, and Father Pecoraro did not mention this to either George or Kathy when leaving the house. But on December 24, 1975, Pecoraro called George Lutz and advised him to stay out of the second floor room where he had heard the mysterious voice (old bedroom of Marc and John DeFeo). However, the call was cut short by static...

Father James Pecoraro, a retired priest of the Diocese of Kansas City - St. Joseph, died on February 24 at Grace Gardens Retirement Community. Father Pecoraro passed just days short of his 92nd birthday which would have been April 3. He was a priest for 55 years.

James Pecoraro was born in Rochester, New York, to Antonio and Fortunata Vallone Pecoraro in 1916.

Father James A. Pecoraro

What followed was a catalogue of terrifying incidents, some of which appeared to relate to the DeFeo murders that had occurred. George would wake up around 3:15 every morning and feel compelled to check the boathouse. Later he would learn that this was the estimated time of the DeFeo killing.

Kathy began having vivid nightmares about the murders and discovered (through dreams) the order in which the murders had occurred and the rooms where they took place.

Their children's behaviour deteriorated and they also began to sleep on their stomachs, in the same way that the dead bodies in the DeFeo murders had been found.

George discovered a small hidden room (around four feet by five feet) behind shelving in the basement. The walls of the room were painted red and the room itself did not appear in the blueprints for the house. known as the "Red Room" the family dog Harry, refused to go anywhere near it and was often seen cowering close by the room as if sensing something to fear was in there.

Other incidents included: swarms of flies in the middle of winter, cold spots and odours of perfume and excrement in the house when there were no drafts or piping to explain the source, and a blood type substance oozed from the walls in the hall and from the keyhole of the playroom door (in the third floor attic room). A 12-inch crucifix which was hanging in the living room was found upside down and began emitting a sour smell. Locks, doors and windows in the house were damaged by unseen forces and on one occasion the family awoke to find their front door (*which I suspect was a screen-door*) had been quite literally torn off its hinges.

George claimed he often heard doors and windows slamming, when there was no one, or no known cause for the sound, but on one occasion, Kathy had opened the window in the master bedroom to "air out the room" and sent Daniel to close it because of a change in the weather. Moments later the boy screamed out in pain as the window slammed closed on its own accord crushing Danny's fingers, which George and Kathy later described as looking flat. They were amazed that none of the bones in the child's hand had been broken.

Newly-Weds George & Kathy Lutz

George Lutz claimed he was regularly woken by the sound of the front door slamming. He would race down-stairs only to find the dog sleeping soundly by the front door.

Nobody else heard the sound although George claimed that it was loud enough to wake the whole household.

George also said he heard what he described as a "German Marching band tuning up" and on other occasions, what sounded like a clock radio playing not quite on frequency, but again, when he went to investigate, the noise would cease.

On one occasion George tripped over an ornamental china lion which they kept in the living-room, and upon inspection of the wound he discovered what he later described as "bite marks" on his ankle.

Kathy Lutz also reported strange occurrences in the house, including: Feeling a sensation of "being embraced" in a loving manner by an unseen force. She also developed red welts on her chest, again caused by an unseen force, and is said to have levitated two-feet off her bed. She was witnessed undergoing what can best be described as a transfiguration and turned from a young woman into an old hag looking around ninety-years of age.

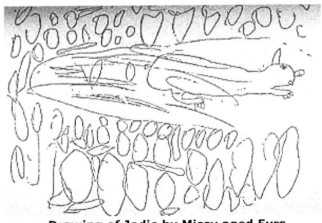

Drawing of Jodie by Missy aged 5yrs

On one cold December night, Kathy noticed that Missy's widow was open and asked her why? The five-year old told her mother that it was open because Jodie had to climb out! When Kathy closed the window she saw what she described as two 'red glowing eyes' staring back at her. On January 1, 1976, they discovered outside house (below Missy's bedroom window), cloven hoof-prints in the snow.

Missy's Bedroom

Lutz sewing room

These freakish events continued on a daily basis and seemed to grow in intensity the longer the family stayed in the house. One day, while tending to the fire, George and Kathy both claimed they saw the image of a demon with half its face blown away burned in to the soot at the back of the fireplace! The couple had tried to tiptoe around the subject for a while, as the cost of the property had been a big financial investment on George's part.

But they quickly realised that there was unquestionably something wrong with their new home, so decided that something had to be done.

On January 8, 1976, George and Kathy attempted to rid the house of its evil influence by walking from room to room holding a silver crucifix while they both recited the Lord's Prayer. Upon entering the living-room George allegedly heard a chorus of voices saying; "Will you stop?"

It didn't stop and at 7am on January 14 1976, after only 28 days of living in the house on Ocean Avenue, George, Kathy, their children and dog Harry, scrambled in to their van and drove away from the house, leaving behind all their possessions.

Describing some of the events of that last night to a journalist for *Stars and Stripes* in in 1980, George said: "It was the accumulation of events all happening at once that made us leave. Beds were actually banging up and down on the floor, furniture was sliding around and drawers were flying back and forth. Doors throughout the house were opening and slamming closed."

Post-Amityville photograph of Father Pecoraro outside Kathy's mothers house with Danny and Christopher Lutz.

"We decided it's our story, this is what happened, we're either going to stand up and say this happened, or we're going to try and become anonymous some-place else.

George Lutz (April 12th 2005)

The Amityville Story Hits the News

As the family had invested all their money in to the purchase of the property they were obviously keen to try and recoup some of their losses so contacted a paranormal investigator who claimed to be a parapsychologist by the name of Stephen Kaplan to help them get rid of whatever was effecting the house.   Kaplan immediately told the press and media that he was going to investigate the Amityville case. This angered the Lutzes who where at that time trying to avoid unwanted publicity. Kaplan also started referring to himself as a "Vampirologist" which did not fill them with confidence in his ability to help them with their particular problem - so declined his offer of help, and started to look elsewhere.

On the night of March 6, 1976, the house was investigated by Ed and Lorraine Warren, accompanied by a New York Channel-5 news team, the reporter Michael Linder of WNEW-FM, and Gene Campbell took a series of infrared time-lapse photographs.   Although he was asked to attend, George Lutz refused but did give the team the keys to the house.

Almost immediately upon entering the building, Ed Warren began experiencing heart palpitations. His wife Lorraine (a clairvoyant) told reporters that she could sense an unearthly presence in the house, and Shinnecock Indians had used the land on which the house stood, as an isolated area for sick and insane members of their tribe. However, she also added that they did not bury their dead at that location because it was "possessed by demons."

The Shinnecock Indian Nation

The Last of the Shinnecock Indians L.I.N.Y. 1864

Once based at the eastern end of Long Island, New York

In January 1977, parapsychologist Hans Holzer also investigated the house along with medium Ethel Meyers, who claimed the house had been built over an ancient Native American burial ground. Holzer documented the investigation, along with an interview with Ronald DeFeo Jr, in his book Murder in Amityville.

Both the Warrens and Holzer always claimed that the house was occupied by malevolent spirits due to its history.

Indian Relics at Amityville.

Amityville, L. I., March 30—Workmen engaged in digging a cellar for a new house to be erected on the property of E. W. Bourdette, on Ocean avenue, in this village, have discovered several skeletons, some of them in a good state of preservation. They are believed to be the remains of Indians of the Iroquois tribe, who long ago had a burying ground in this vicinity. On the same property, which up to a few years ago was only an immense mound of clam and oyster shells, trees have been found which are believed to have been set out by this same tribe. They are peculiar in their growth, foliage and the nature of the wood, the species of which no one in this locality can identify. The Iroquois owned vast tracts of land in this vicinity and at Woodsburgh on the Far Rockaway branch of the Long Island railroad, is a monument erected to one of the chiefs of the Iroquois on land formerly owned by him. The stone commemorates a life long friendship between Cululoo and Abram Hewlett, the purchaser of the ground on which the Indian lived.

THE BROOKLYN DAILY EAGLE
SATURDAY, MARCH 30, 1895

Indian Relics at Amityville.

Amityville, L.I., March 30 - Workmen engaged in digging a cellar for a new house to be erected on the property of E. W. Bourdette, on Ocean Avenue in the village, have discovered several skeletons, some of them in a good state of preservation. They are believed to be the remains of Indians of the Iroquois Tribe, who long ago had a burying ground in the vicinity. On the same property, which up to a few years ago was only an immense mound of clam and oyster shells, trees have been found which are believed to have been set out by this same tribe. They are peculiar in their growth, foliage and the nature of the wood, the species of which no one in this locality can identify. The Iroquois owned vast tracts of land in this vicinity and at Woodsburgh on the far Rockaway branch of the Long Island rail-road, is a monument erected to one of the chiefs of the Iroquois on the land formerly owned by him. The stone commemorates a life long friendship between Cululoo and Abram Hewlett, the purchaser of the ground on which the Indian lived.

It was the initial investigation which began the media frenzy that eventually resulted in Stephen Kaplan (who seemed furious at being turned down by the Lutzes) contacting a Long Island newspaper, telling them that he believes the haunting was nothing more than a hoax – which is a brave statement from someone who classed himself as a *Vampirologist*... And this is where things got really complicated.

Kaplan began what could best be described as a media hate campaign against the Lutz family, and would frequently appear on television and radio voicing his opinions in the late 1970s and 80s.

This raised his profile and made him a household name for a short time, and he eventually wrote a book titled *The Amityville Horror Conspiracy* along with his wife Roxanne Salch Kaplan.

But nothing is ever straightforward when it comes to the house on Ocean Avenue, and somewhat ironically, the same year his book was published (1995), Stephen Kaplan died of a heart attack weeks before the book was released.

With hindsight, it seems obvious that Dr Stephen Kaplan had alternative motives for trying to debunk the case. Maybe greed, or just foolish pride – or perhaps he just started believing his own hype? Whatever his motives, I would take his statements about the haunting with a pinch of salt... Even his claim to a PhD is questionable?

However, the damaging mud from Kaplan's hate campaign stuck! And Father Ralph J Pecoraro (the Roman Catholic Priest who blessed the house) had his reputation dragged through the mud, and the Lutz family were branded as liars in the press and on various television chat shows.

Stephen Kaplan - Vampirologist

Many were quick to jump on the *sceptic* bandwagon, claiming that if the incidents Lutzes described were true, then why did the family not just simply call in the police? Some even said that the Lutz family returned days after they fled the house to conduct a garage sale – which is utterly untrue! Many others pointed their fingers at the Lutzes, believing that they made up the whole story as some sort of money making strategy. But historically, nobody previous *or since* has ever become rich over a claimed haunted house?

The real fact is that at that time, nobody knew the book would take-off with the public, become a bestseller and be made in to a movie.

Furthermore, if this is to be considered as a motive for the Lutzes claims, then surely they would have ensured that they got well paid from these ventures?

The reality is that the author, Jay Anson and the film producers became millionaires. The Lutzes on the other hand, made very little in comparison. George later told the makers of the *History's Mysteries* documentary, that he estimates they made approximately $250,000 from the book and $160,000 from the film.

Sceptics also claimed that George was having financial problems and couldn't afford to pay for the house – But again, the fact is that George's company was doing well, and he had no problem whatsoever getting the mortgage for 112 Ocean Avenue. In fact he got his mortgage from the first bank he applied to.

"The Lutzes did seem like a pretty normal family. Very normal. Very loving. And that's what made their experience all the more horrifying."

Lorraine Warren

Ghost Boy?

The photograph above was taken inside the house on Ocean Avenue during the original Ed and Lorraine Warren investigation of March 6, 1976. It was captured by Gene Campbell, a professional photographer who had set up an automatic camera (that took infrared pictures) to cover the second floor landing during the nights vigil.

The Photograph captured what appears to be a young boy with glowing eyes who is looking out of a doorway directly towards the camera.

George and Kathy Lutz revealed the photograph in 1979, (three years after it was taken), when they appeared on The Merv Griffin Show, along with Rod Steiger to promote the release of the first movie. Some have speculated that the image could be the ghost of the murdered child, John DeFeo.

41

Shiny Eyed Ghost Boy Close Up

Ghost Boy? Photographer by Gene Campbell

This photograph has been cited as one of the best pieces of evidence ever produced. And certainly does look very spooky...

But many sceptics, and supporters of the Lutzes, think that the *Ghost Boy* is probably one of the investigators working with the Warrens during the initial investigation called Paul Bartz. The ghostly glow in the eyes being either due to the infrared film, or more probably a pair of spectacles worn at that time. They both seem to be wearing very similar shirts!

Paul Bartz on the night of the investigation

"COPE??? I didn't have a choice! I was just a kid back then, where was I going to go?"

Christopher Quaratino (AKA Chris Lutz)

Christopher Quaratino
(AKA Chris Lutz)

After thirty-five years of living in the shadow of the worlds most famous haunted house, Christopher Quaratino (aka Christopher Lutz) decided to step out of the shadows and address the subject which has haunted him all his life. The following interviews were conducted and compiled with the help of Christopher both online and telephone conversations in 2011.

MH: Do you remember much about your time living on Ocean Avenue, and what where your thoughts about the bad press that followed?

Chris: I was only 8 years old when we moved out of that house and yes I was terrified, but obviously I had no say in all the media hype that followed. The simple fact is that I lived through the true events, both inside the house and afterwards and nothing that had been put in movies or published to date comes close to what really happened.

MH: What do you think of the film-makers exploiting your families misfortunes?

Chris: I don't have much control over what the Hollywood film-makers do. They make these outlandish movies and try and pass it off as being part of the True Story, which none of them are.

MH: I have to admit that I really enjoyed the original 1979 film based on Jay Anson's novel and staring James Brolin and Margot Kidder as George and Kathy Lutz and always thought it gave a sort of accurate account of what took place in the house. How do you rate the movie?

Chris: To be honest, I really get embarrassed about that film! Especially when I operated a machine gun in the 10TH Mountain Division during the first gulf war. This was a rough time for me and for all of us, but we became very close as a squad and I felt like I belonged.
We were all willing to put our lives on the line for each other, which is something that truly brings people together and for one of the first times in my life I felt like I was no different to anyone else in my platoon and didn't stand out.
But one day they screened The Amityville Horror movie in the barracks, and suddenly everyone seemed to want to sit and watch it with me. It was really embarrassing!

MH: I read an interview given by George Lutz following the release of the book in which he stated that Jay Anson's book: "tells it pretty much the way it happened, although we asked that some things be kept out. There are some things that happened which we won't tell anyone about." Do you know what George was referring to?

Chris: Where did you see this quote you refer to?

MH: The quote came from Stars and Stripes and was written by George H Roberts Jr - published March 26, 1980.

Chris: I just find what George said then to be very telling – that there was more information. Yet that begs the question of why he held the information back? To me the stuff withheld is what puts the blame on him and not solely the house. Anson's book paints George as a victim of the house and a hero to the family, rescuing us in the end, when the real story is that he was practising the occult and called it up himself. This is the main reason I am doing this, so the real story can be told, and to address the false stories which have been flying around.

MH: Wow! It seems strange that George would hint at that then? So George was in to the occult? That really does put a new twist on Anson's book.

Chris: A major twist. That is why it followed us – He called it up! In real life, just as in book The Amityville Horror part-2, George needed an exorcism. You don't need an exorcism because you live in a haunted house... You get an exorcism because you have demons.

MH: I read book two and three many years ago and remember thinking it was strange that 'it' seemed to follow you after leaving the house, but now it makes perfect sense. It must have been terrifying for you growing up with this going on. Did the exorcism work? And how did you all cope living with George's demon?

Chris: COPE??? ... I didn't have a choice! I was just a kid back then, where was I going to go? Are you familiar with what the Bible says about a man whose demons get cast out – what happens to that man afterwards?

MH: I see what you mean! I assume you are referring to MATTHEW verse 12 – 43 to 45. When cast out it goes and brings with it seven other spirits more evil than itself

Chris: I'll let the fruit of his life be what people judge. Was it good fruit or bad fruit? What sort of tree was George – good or bad? We aren't to judge... but we are to be fruit inspectors.

MH: I really admire your philosophy and I must admit that I am starting to see that the house itself was just the tip of the iceberg. So why do you think that after all these years and after all the nonsense that has been added to the story, that it keeps coming back and keeps getting retold?

Chris: I think the answer to that is simple. Although the events have been exaggerated and made more sensational by the movie makers and over-enthusiastic writers, the story keeps returning because people can tell that there are roots of truth buried beneath the surface. I want to tell the real story about what happened, but every time something appears in the press someone just uses it. If I was to tell you everything now, it would be twisted and used by someone else before I got the chance to give the TRUE version, and I don't want that to happen.

MH: I can fully understand your reasoning, and look forward to reading your full account for myself one day.

Chris: My main problem at the moment is when I sit looking at the blank plasma screen, the words just will not come. I can only tell my story when I'm with someone who has not heard it before. Maybe that's what I will do. I'll record myself telling the story and have it translated in to text. I will give you another interview once my story has been told, and I will give you a full run-down of everything I have experienced.

"Before my eyes she began to change into an old lady with grey hair..."

George Lutz

During my conversation with Christopher I mentioned a quote by George Lutz which I had read in *Stars and Stripes*. This was an interview conducted by the Journalist George H. Roberts Jr, first published on March 26th 1980. Chris had not head of this, and seemed surprised at some of the answers. The following is a transcript of the article:

While on a visit to Tokyo in 1980, George and Kathleen Lutz talked about their experiences in the "Amityville Horror" house.

TOKYO -- After 28 days of terror George Lutz and his family were forced to flee the home of their dreams, convinced it housed evil spirits.

"I never believed in the supernatural, or anything other than God. But I had also never experienced the ultimate terror that we lived with in that house," said George Lutz.

He was in Japan with his wife, Kathleen, recently to promote the Tokyo premier of a movie based on their experiences in the large colonial house at 112 Ocean Ave., Amityville, N.Y., the scene of a mass murder.

On Nov. 13,1974, 24-year-old Ronald DeFeo took a high-powered rifle and methodically shot his parents, two brothers and two sisters.

"At first," said Mrs. Lutz, "Police were testing for drugs. They thought he might have drugged his sleeping family before killing them. He fired eight shots to kill six people and not one of them woke up during it.

"We were told about the murder just before we purchased the house," said Mrs. Lutz, "but we didn't think much about it."

After paying $80,000, the Lutzes, along with their three children, Missy, 5, Dan, 9, and Chris, 7, moved into their dream home on Dec. 18, 1975.

"It had everything we wanted," said Lutz, "a swimming pool, lots of room, a full basement, and it was close to the water with a boat house for my cabin cruiser.

"But things started happening from the day we moved into the place," he said.

"It began with the heating system. Although it had been checked out and certified, we could never get it to produce heat. It seemed to always stay around 50 degrees. Kathy would be in the kitchen and feel somebody touch her. Light at first, then as time went on it would become harder and she would pass out.

"There was the smell of cheap perfume. Doors would open and close. Whatever you did in a room would be undone when you came back to it. If you made the bed, it would be pulled apart when you came back, and objects would move around.

Lutz said they called a Catholic priest to bless their new home. "As he began the ceremony he felt something slap his face and heard a masculine voice say 'GET OUT!'"

After the priest left he was driving down the highway and felt his car being pulled toward the right. He stopped and checked it. Finding nothing wrong he continued on his way. Without warning the hood flew off his car. He called another priest who drove him to the rectory.

"So many things were happening at the same time, it began to be hard to keep up with them," said Lutz. "We finally ended up buying a tape recorder and recording all our experiences.

"There would be voices, music, a strange green Jell-O-like substance that oozed out of the walls and floor. Our daughter Missy began to play with an invisible pig named Jodie. We began to wake up at 3:15 in the morning and Kathy would have these pains in her back and head.

"On checking with the police we found that we were able to tell them things about the murders that nobody except the police knew. We learned that the murders had occurred at 3:15am, that the mother had been shot in the back and head where Kathy felt the pain. And we were able to tell the police the positions of the bodies when they were found, as the children and Kathy began waking up in the same positions.

"The first officer at the murder scene had also complained about the smell of cheap perfume. One night I woke up and looked at Kathy, who was still asleep," said Lutz. "Before my eyes she began to change into an old lady with grey hair and all. Then she began to raise up into the air. She was just floating there for a while. Then she woke up and caught a glimpse of herself in the mirror and began to scream."

Repeated levitations became commonplace in the house along with manifestations of a little boy asking for help, a hooded figure, the entity named Jodie, the cheap perfume smell and a mass of flies in the sewing room.

"It was the accumulation of events all happening at once that made us leave," Lutz continued. "Beds were actually banging up and down on the floor, furniture was sliding around and drawers were flying back and forth. Doors throughout the house were opening and slamming closed."

The Lutz family lasted 28 days in the house at 112 Ocean Ave. At 7 am. on Jan. 14, 1976, the Lutzes ran to their van, leaving behind all their clothes, furniture and possessions.

Even after fleeing to Kathy's mother's home, the couple would wake to find themselves levitating.

"There we were wide awake, both of us floating in the air. I was saying, can you believe this, can you believe what's happening to us," Lutz said.

"People ask me why I stayed in the house as long as I did," Lutz said. "But the house had a strange comfort to it. Once you were inside, you did not want to leave. It was, after all, our home. Yet it affected everyone who entered it."

The Shinnecock Indians were said to have used the land the house was built on to pen their mad, sick and dying until they died of exposure. Later, a male witch forced from Salem, Mass., reportedly set up shop there.

The house, built in 1928, was home for several families. All of them suffered financial or family difficulties, Mr. Lutz said.

The Lutzes told their story in a book titled "The Amityville Horror." The book, written by Jay Anson, sold a quarter of a million copies, but the Lutzes said they still have not regained what they lost when they abandoned the house.

Anson recently died of a heart attack. While working on the book with him, one of his secretaries died, another was injured in a car accident and the thirds home caught fire, Lutz said.

"The book," said Lutz, "tells it pretty much the way it happened, although we asked that some things be kept out. There are some things that happened which we won't tell anyone about."

The book is now a movie of the same name.

"I'd like to say that the movie is based on our experiences because, after all, it is Hollywood. Some things are done for effect, but all the emotions are there. Then, too, some of the happenings were worse than the movie."

According to Lutz, the events experienced by him and his family are not as rare as one would believe.

"We have been told by experts in this field that many normal people experience cold spots in certain rooms and tend to avoid certain areas of the house, or just close off the room and forget it. They are worried about what others will say. I feel that there is some physical evil form, and that it can be dangerous."

"All the people who come to us are crazy"

Ed Warren

Above: George Lutz near the Pool of 112 Ocean Avenue. Possibly the only Photo of him taken while he and his family were living at the house.

HIGH HOPES

While it is true that George Lutz always claimed to have no prior knowledge of the occult or paranormal until after they left the house on Ocean Avenue, Chris told me that his stepfather was in fact a friend of Raymond Buckland and had been interested in the occult for some years – long before they moved into the house and long before he met his mother Kathy.

Raymond Buckland was born in London in 1934 and emigrated to the United States in 1962, where he lived in Long Island, New York, which coincidentally (or not) is not too far away from the Amityville house. Buckland always had an interest in witchcraft and the occult, and was a practitioner of the arts. He started corresponding with Gerald Gardner (the Father of modern witchcraft) in the Isle of Man.

The two became good friends and had many telephone conversations, which resulted in Buckland becoming Gardner's spokesman in America. Buckland travelled to Scotland with Gardner where he was initiated into the craft by the High Priestess Monique Wilson, and upon returning to America, Buckland founded a coven known as the Long Island Coven.

The group followed the Gardnerian Wicca lineage but tried to keep their identities secret. Unfortunately for those concerned, journalist Lisa Hoffman of the New York Sunday News published a story about them, without their permission, which is possibly where George Lutz first became aware of Buckland.

In 1968, Raymond Buckland founded the first Museum of Witchcraft and Magic in the United States, which was heavily influenced by Gardner's Museum of Witchcraft and Magic.

Visitors to the Museum were initially by appointment only and the museum itself was located in Buckland's own basement.

However, as the collection of artefacts grew he moved the museum to a 19TH century house in Bay Shore where it received quite a bit of media attention and even a documentary was made about it. In 1973, Raymond separated from his wife Rosemary and moved his museum to Weirds Beach in New Hampshire.

Above: Raymond Buckland - founder of America's first Museum of Witchcraft and Magic

If Chris Lutz is correct, then George is said to have visited the museum on a number of occasions prior to it being moved in 1973.

If indeed a friend of Buckland, then George might have had enough knowledge on the subject to either '*provoke*' something or possibly even to '*hoax*' something.

Chris is one hundred percent adamant that his stepfather provoked something in the Amityville house but whatever it was he did 'call-up' was not haunting the house but George himself, which is why it followed him once they had left the property.

This may also help to explain why subsequent owners of the house do not report similar occurrences happening to them.

I tried to find something to corroborate the claims made by Chris and although it took a while to find, I discovered a passage in Stephen Kaplan's book *The Amityville Horror Conspiracy* (1995), which fully supports this.

In a discussion about witchcraft George Lutz mentions Ray Buckland, and Kapaln asks: "Oh, you've heard of Ray Buckland?" George replies: "Sure I knew Ray; we had some interesting conversations about witchcraft when he ran the museum."

It is interesting to note that if you tried a Google search for this information (at the time of writing the original article for Psychic World Newspaper) a number of sites showed-up but when I clicked on these sites, I found they had all been 'suspended'.

If this new information is correct then it finally explains many of the inconsistencies which have surrounded the Amityville haunting, such as why the haunting followed the family and why other owners of the house were not troubled with the same phenomena. It may even be possible that George Lutz himself had some mediumistic gift and may not have even realised it and armed with his small knowledge of witchcraft and living in a house where such tragedies had occurred, I am sure the atmosphere could become very overwhelming for the unwary.

Whatever the cause, Chris, his brother Danny and sister Missy are united in their beliefs that something took place in that house, and whatever it was continued to follow them long after they left.

~

"I didn't want to be the Amityville horror kid. I've been running away from it my whole life and it finally caught up with me."

Daniel Lutz (March 8th 2013)

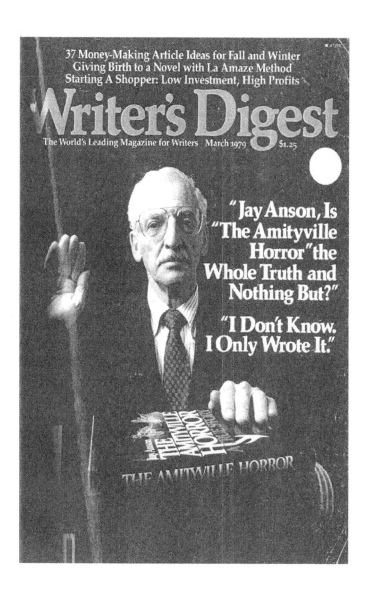

37 Money-Making Article Ideas for Fall and Winter
Giving Birth to a Novel with La Amaze Method
Starting A Shopper: Low Investment, High Profits

Writer's Digest

The World's Leading Magazine for Writers   March 1979 $1.25

"Jay Anson, Is
"The Amityville
Horror"the
Whole Truth and
Nothing But?"

"I Don't Know.
I Only Wrote It."

THE AMITYVILLE HORROR

Some Facts V Some Fiction

Kathleen Theresa Lutz died of emphysema (October 13, 1946 – August 17, 2004). George Lee Lutz (January 1, 1947 – May 8, 2006) died of heart disease.

The couple divorced in the late 1980s, but remained on good terms, and to the very end they were in total agreement that events they described taking place at Amityville were all true.

In support of George and Kathy, I feel I should remind readers that they both underwent questioning while taking a polygraph tests. Although 100% accurate, Frank Horvath of the *American Polygraph Association* tells us:

"Proponents will say the test is about 90 percent accurate. Critics will say it's about 70 percent accurate."

Prior to the Lutzes test, many people had been caught-out '*lying*' - from alien abductees to killers. George and Kathy were tests by Chris Gugas and Michael Rice, who were among the top five experts in the country for conducting polygraph tests. Gugas reportedly taught the FBI how to use them!

Muddying the water further, Sceptic claimed that the tests were conducted by the *Star* tabloid as a publicity stunt, which is untrue. And while it is true that *American International Pictures* (who made the movie) wanted the tests done, and I suspect had publicity at the forefront of their minds, the Lutzes agreed to this *only* if the most qualified people performed the tests. And that is who they got.

There is no question in my mind that the Lutz family experienced *something* in that house that none of them could explain – but many of the things attributed to the haunting *can* easily dismissed.

For example, the *red room* which didn't show-up on the house plans, was almost certainly a result of the original building being moved and the new house being built over its foundations.

The movies and books twisted this part of the tale turning the room it into a *gateway to hell*.

I am sure that the Lutzes where surprised to find the room, and quite understandably could not explain a reason for its existence at that time, the simple fact is, it was nothing more that a storage space used by the DeFeo children to store their toys. In more resent times the new owner redesigned the basement in the house, and the room was built over – so now no longer exits.

Although I site the original book The Amityville Horror as the inspiration for becoming a researcher and now Assistant Editor of Psychic World Newspaper (*the book is such a good read*), but I fully acknowledge that there are many discrepancies in Jay Anson's script. This is partly due to the Lutzes themselves, who despite numerous requested from Anderson, refused to be interviewed claiming it would be "too painful" and they did not want to relive their experiences again. They just wanted to put the past in the past and try to move on with their lives.

They did however gave Anson all their recordings which they made after leaving the house. These recordings where made by Kathy and George as they remembered incidents, but were in no particular order.

While it is true that Jay Anson was granted interviews with other people involved with the family during the time they spent in the house, these witnesses and associates did not have full knowledge of the Lutzes experiences, and certainly did not know all the details of every day the family spent in that house.

The inconsistencies in the book were address by Anson in the publication *Writer's Digest* (March 1979 issue), but it was a little half hearted, claiming: "Yeah, I know the psychical research people say I have made mistakes. They say that on *such and such* a day when I said it rained, it didn't rain. So what? I am a perfectly normal human being, and sometimes I make mistakes."

Unfortunately, and somewhat sadly, Jay Anson didn't get much of a chance to defend his work, as a year later (March 12, 1980) he died at the young aged 58

Much of the confusion over *facts* concerning the Lutz family's experiences on Ocean Avenue can be blamed on the people with Ronald DeFeo Junior and the original murders, such as William Weber who defends Ronnie DeFeo in court.

Following the trial Weber planed to write a book about the case and hired Paul Hoffman to write it. The deadline for the completion of the manuscript was set for the end of 1976.

George and Kathy Lutz meet with Weber, who originally wants their story included in his book. Although George and Kathy may have indicated that they would be willing to do this, they eventually decide against Weber's deal after discovering that Ronald DeFeo Junior would have been one of the parties who would have benefited from the royalties.

As we all know, the Original Amityville Horror book was written by Jay Anson.   However, Weber made claims that some of Anson's story was concocted by himself and the Lutzes (which has never been proven).

Paul Hoffman then wrote an article about the haunting for the New York Daily News, which was based on his earlier conversations with the Lutzes prior to them declining the deal.   But Hoffman failed to do his version of the book, so Hans Holzer was approached by Weber in the latter part of 1976, and started investigating the Amityville case from the DeFeo perspective.

This started a rivalry between Holzer and Hoffman, who still wants to write Weber's book, so he resold his earlier NY Daily News story to *Good Housekeeping* magazine, and ended-up owing Weber and DeFeo a percentage of the fee he received from the venture.

Eventually it was Holzer who managed complete the book for Weber (based upon the murders rather than the haunting), titled *Murder in Amityville*.   The rights of the book were later sold and formed the basis for the movie *Amityville II*, which again Weber is said to have gotten a percentage from.

Murder in Amityville contains and interview Holzer did with DeFeo while in prison, along with an investigation in to the haunting at the house on Ocean Avenue, which was conducted by the author and medium Ethel Meyers. This investigation very heavily suggests that Ronald DeFeo was possessed at the time he committed the murders... But in a letter written by DeFeo on May 1st 2000, he states that he (and two other people), had committed the crime, saying:

"...it was cold-blooded murder. Period. No ghosts. No demons. Just three people in which I was one."

It is also interesting to note that the authorities in Amityville, New York, were very keen to play-down the whole incident, and regularly decline requests to discuss the events publicly. The website of the Amityville Historical Society has no mention of the murders committed by Ronald DeFeo Jr, or the the Lutz family's time living at 112 Ocean Avenue. And when the History Channel made their documentary about The Amityville Horror (in 2000), none of the staff member of the Historical Society would discuss the matter on camera.

With this in mind, it was also suggested by many who were eager to keep the mystery of the Amityville mythology alive that when *American International Pictures* wanted to film the movie *The Amityville Horror,* that they could not use the real house because the film crew were too scared to go in there. But the truth is that because of the damage caused by Kaplan's media hate campaign, most of the Villagers living in Amityville (and the authorities) viewed the haunting a hoax and did not want their quiet community dragged in to the media any further. Thus *American International Pictures* were denied shooting permits.

~

Final Word

No matter what your take on the Amityville Horror, one thing is certain... Both George and Kathy Lutz died still claiming that their experiences in Amityville were real. And even if Christopher and Daniel are correct in their belief that the stepfather George was the cause, it was still a Horror for all who had to endure it!

I think Kathleen Lutz explained her views best during an interview for the History Channel in 2000:

"Some people have called our testimony about Amityville a hoax. There is nothing that I could say to them... There is nothing I could show them that would be new evidence that this is the truth. It is the truth. It is my testimony. It is where I came from. And to judge another's testimony, not having experienced it, not having gone through it, or been touched by it... You don't have the right to. Yours is just an opinion... And the opinion doesn't hold water."

71

INSIDE THE AMITYVILLE HOUSE

Front Door Entrance

TV Room (P1)

TV Room (P2)

Dinning Room (P1)

Dinning Room (P2)

Kitchen Breakfast Nook

Kitchen

Hallway Bottom of the Stairs

Stairs to the First Floor

Bedroom of Dawn DeFeo

Bedroom of Dawn (2)

John Matthew and Marc Gregory Bedroom

**John Matthew and Marc Gregory
Bedroom (Pic:2)**

Bedroom of Alison (1)

Bedroom of Alison (2)

Master Bedroom (P1)

Master Bedroom (P2)

Second Floor Looking up

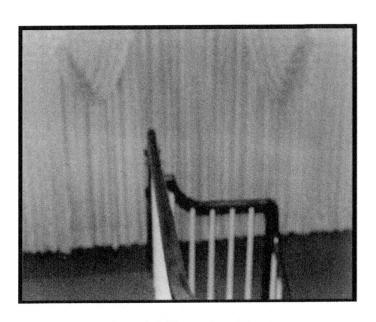

Second Floor Landing

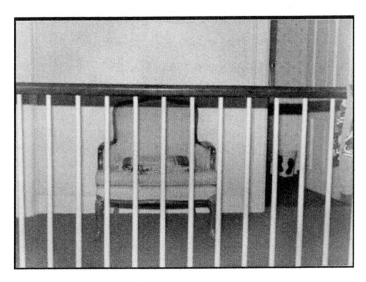

Third Floor Landing

Third Floor Bedroom (Ronald DeFeo Jr)

Third Floor Bedroom (Ronald DeFeo Jr)

Basement Stairs

Basement Room (p1)

Basement Room (p2)

The Night of the DeFeo Murders

The original house 112 Ocean Avenue, still exists but it has been renovated and the address changed in order to discourage sightseers from visiting it. The famous quarter moon windows have been removed and the house today looks considerably different from the way it has been depicted in the movies.

The House as it looks today

The house used in the original three movies (Toms River location) has also been modified for the same reason. Although it was originally altered for the part in the movies, it is now back in (more or less) its original form.

The iconic house as it appears in the first three movies

Further Reading

The Amityville Horror
by Jay Anson

The original, and probably the best book written about the house on Ocean Avenue, and the Lutz family's time living in Amityville.   Sceptic, believer or just a fan of horror – this book will keep you happy to the last page.

~

The Amityville Horror Part II
by John G. Jones

The Amityville Horror Part II is a book written by John G. Jones as the sequel to The Amityville Horror. The book was published in 1982 and recounts the aftermath of the original book and what happened to the Lutzes after they fled 112 Ocean Avenue.

~

Murder in Amityville
by Hans Holzer

Murder In Amityville serves as a prequel to The Amityville Horror, and is credited with being the main influence for the movie titled Amityville II: The Possession

**High Hopes: The Amityville Murders
by Gerard Sullivan and Harvey Aronson**

Relates the true story of the 1974 Amityville murder of six members of the DeFeo family and the ensuing investigation and trial of Ron DeFeo for the crime.

~

Amityville: The Final Chapter
by John G. Jones

Amityville: The Evil Escapes
by John G. Jones

The Amityville Curse
by Hans Holzer

Amityville: The Horror Returns
by John G. Jones

Amityville: The Nightmare Continues
by Robin Karl

Books by Matthew Hutton

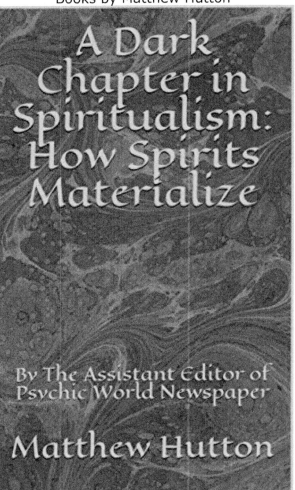

A Dark Chapter in Spiritualism: *How Spirits Materialize*
An investigation in to fraudulent mediumship
conducted in 1907

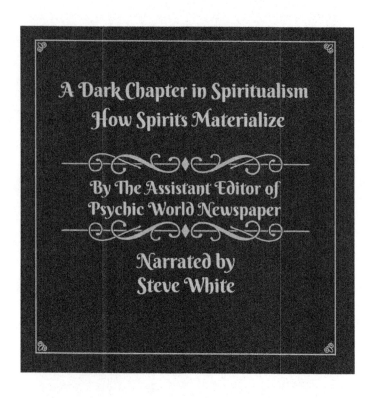

A Dark Chapter in Spiritualism: *How Spirits Materialize*
Audio Book version of an investigation in to fraudulent mediumship conducted in 1907. Narrated by Voice Actor Steve White who is best known for his *Strange but True Stories*

The Hylton Castle Ghost

By the Assistant Editor of Psychic World Newspaper

Matthew Hutton

The Hylton Castle Ghost

In the north of County Durham stands Hylton Castle. It was home to one of the oldest, richest and unquestionably one of the most powerful families in the history of County Durham. It also has the reputation of being one of the most haunted homes in England. First published by Island Light (Dec. 1999), the 'Hylton Castle Ghost' is a true account of an investigation conducted at the Hylton Castle on October 19th 1989. Printed in large format and print for partially sighted readers

The Living Ghosts of Prudhoe Castle
A True Short Story

True account of families living in a haunted castle during the 1950s, along with an investigation in the 90s, and the continued sightings.

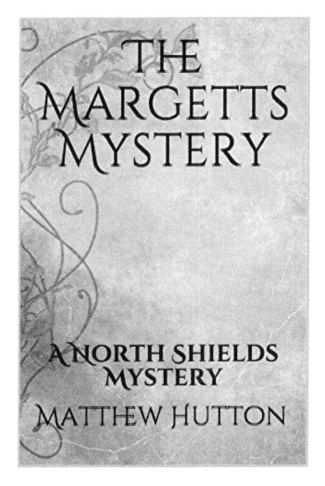

THE MARGETTS MYSTERY

A NORTH SHIELDS MYSTERY

MATTHEW HUTTON

In the first part of the 19th century, many young men held a secret longing to abandon their lives in North Shields, along with their homes and families, and sail away to distant lands in search of wealth, romance and adventure... John Margetts was not one of them! He disappeared one night under the most unnatural circumstances.

Haunted Gateshead

A Brief Guide to a Ghostly Past

Matthew Hutton

Haunted Gateshead

After a visit to Gateshead in 1933, the author and playwright, J. B. Priestley, wrote: "The whole town appeared to have been carefully planned by an enemy of the human race."

However, residents seem very reluctant to leave the town... Even after death!

Mysteries Ghosts and Aliens

Tales from Psychic World Newspaper

Matthew Hutton

Mysteries Ghosts and Aliens
A collection of the best articles from Psychic
World Newspaper from the past twenty years

101

The Spectral Guide to Tyneside
Haunted locations and local legends from around
the North East of England. Most of the locations
mentioned in the book are open to the public,
making it a useful guide for wannabe Ghost
Hunters and tourists.

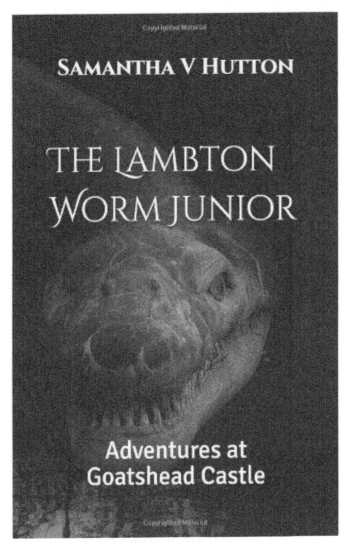

SAMANTHA V HUTTON

THE LAMBTON
WORM JUNIOR

Adventures at
Goatshead Castle

The Lambton Worm Junior
(Audio Version only)
A comedy based upon the Samantha V Hutton
Radio Show. Soon to be an animated series of
the same name. Not for younger children.

After four years on radio, the characters of Goatshead Castle are now taking the world of literature by storm in this comedic Halloween tale! Staring the witch, known as Samantha V Hutton, who is preparing for her annual Halloween ball, with little to no help from her cousin Amanda, her butler Jeeves or the the Lambton Worm Junior, who all seem more interested in telling their stories. Join the Goatshead Castle gang on this comic Halloween adventure full of ghosts, mysteries and very peculiar characters with dark deeds in mind. Be warned – Goatshead Castle is a strange place full of strange people and even stranger beasts! But none more stranger than the Castle maid!

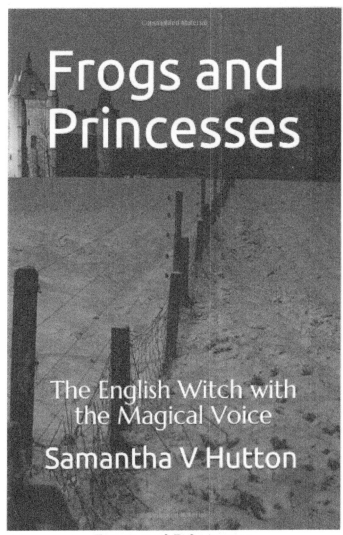

Frogs and

Princesses

The English Witch with the Magical Voice

Samantha V Hutton

Frogs and Princesses
(Audio Version Only)
Seven bedtime stories for younger children.
Based upon the Samantha V Hutton Radio Show.

Printed in Great Britain
by Amazon